T0020611

A World in Need

Down-to-Earth
Prayers of Intercession

Nick Fawcett

Augsburg Books

MINNEAPOLIS

A WORLD IN NEED
Down-to-Earth Prayers of Intercession

Copyright © 2007 Nick Fawcett
Original edition published in English under the title A WORLD IN
NEED by Kevin Mayhew Ltd, Buxhall, England.
This edition copyright © Fortress Press 2019

The prayers in this book previously appeared in *Touching Down,
Heaven Touching Earth, Touched by His Hand,* and *Touching the
Seasons.*

Cover image: Cover art from book interior
Cover design: Tory Herman

Print ISBN: 978-1-5064-5907-3

Contents

Introduction

Few would dispute today that the world is in a mess, perhaps more so than ever before. We've seen positive developments, of course—an end to the Cold War, demolition of the Berlin Wall, peace in Northern Ireland, and the dismantling of Apartheid, to name but some—but these have been replaced by new concerns such as terrorism, climate change, and HIV/AIDS. Add to these natural disasters such as the 2004 tsunami in Indonesia, and the all-too-familiar issues of poverty, injustice, war, and corruption and it's hard to know where to turn for answers.

For Christians, part of the answer is prayer, but though the desire to pray may be there, sometimes the words are not. Perhaps we're unsure what to ask for, perhaps we're unable to express ourselves, or perhaps our good intentions simply get crowded out in the daily routine of life.

Whatever the problem, this book aims to provide a solution. Drawing on four of my recent publications, it shows how prayer can be inspired precisely by that daily routine, God challenging us through such familiar things as a broken window, bowl of soup, suitcase, or jigsaw puzzle. Human need is all around us, calling for our response and speaking of yet wider issues, if only we're ready to look and listen. And, just as God speaks through the ordinary, so no special words are needed to respond. Indeed, it is not finally the words of our prayer that matter so much as the actions to which they lead. My hope is that this book may help inspire both.

Nick Fawcett

The Shoe Store

There were hundreds there,
shoes of every shape and size—
sandals,
boots,
trainers,
stilettos—
a stunning selection of footwear,
suitable for male and female, young and old.
And as I browsed along the shelves,
I found myself thinking of all who would
wear them,
the assortment of people whose feet they'd adorn
in days to come.

Help me, Lord, to put myself
into the shoes of those around me—
not literally,
but in spirit—
for only then can I hope to understand them,
to grasp what makes them tick
and make sense of their experiences,
empathizing with their hopes and fears,
joys and sorrows.
Teach me to look beyond my limited horizons
and narrow interests,
and to identify more fully with others,
as you have identified yourself so wonderfully
with me
and with all.
Amen.

The Test Tube

It reminded me of childhood experiments—
cocktails of chemicals simmering over a Bunsen
burner
and litmus paper testing strange solutions—
but it spoke also of complex research,
of scientists unravelling the mysteries of life,
creating new drugs,
fertilizing eggs,
and identifying genes—
unlocking secrets undreamed of in years gone by.

Such powers, Lord, scare but excite me—
they have potential for both good and evil,
able to enrich life or undermine it,
to transform yet destroy.
Give wisdom to all scientists and researchers,
and to those who set laws regulating
their activities,
so that the skills you have given
may be used responsibly
and to the good of all.
Amen.

The Movie Theater

They watched enthralled,
transported to another world,
sharing the pain and passion of those on screen,
eyes now bright,
now wide with fear,
now filled with tears.
But then it ended—
the spell broken,
characters left behind—
and they returned to the reassuring world of reality,
the scenes that had so recently engrossed them
soon forgotten,
left behind.

Lord, I see other scenes day after day,
images in the news of hunger, squalor, violence,
and suffering
beamed into my living room from across the world,
and my heart goes out to those enduring
such misery.
But once more I can walk away,
leaving it all behind.
Only there's no such leaving for them:
this is their reality.
Remind me, Lord, that they are real people,
each one my neighbor,
and instead of pushing them aside,
as if they were part of another world,
teach me, whenever and wherever I can,
to respond in love.
Amen.

The Bananas

There were hundreds of them,
bunch upon bunch
piled high on the supermarket shelf,
and, with barely a second thought,
a succession of shoppers grabbed a handful,
pausing only to check the quality
before adding some to their shopping cart.

I know, Lord, for I was one of them,
eagerly filling my basket in turn,
yet in each bunch,
had I ears to hear,
you were speaking:
of justice and injustice,
trade and commerce,
toil and effort,
sweat and tears—
of the interdependence of humankind
and the complex web of life.
Remind me each day
of what I owe to others, near and far,
and the many ways they enrich my life.
Remind me of the breadth and wonder of creation
and my responsibilities toward all.
Amen.

The Internet Chat Room

They chatted together,
an astonishing assortment of ages, cultures,
creeds, and backgrounds,
in so many ways miles apart,
yet, thanks to modern technology, brought close,
as though they were there together in one room.

Overcome, Lord, the barriers that keep us apart,
dividing person from person
and race from race—
East and West,
black and white,
male and female,
rich and poor.
Whatever our color, culture, or creed,
draw us together and heal our wounds—
so that we may live and work together as one
people,
one world.
Amen.

The G8 Summit

They carried the world's hopes on their shoulders,
a heavy load to bear,
for though their citizens clamored for change—
wrongs put right
and justice done—
they knew all too well that those same people
would swiftly protest
should change prove costly,
meaning *real* change,
not just for others
but for them.

Lord, I know that if evils are to be tackled
it needs the will of politicians,
governments, and leaders,
and I pray that they'll do their part.
I know it needs fairer trade and relief of debt
coupled with generous, genuine aid,
and I pray these will be achieved.
But save me from using all this to pass the buck
as though the ills of this world are not also down
to me.
As well as *calling* for change,
help me to change in turn,
ready to play *my* part
before I ask others to play *theirs*.
Amen.

The Famine

They were shocking pictures,
indescribably awful—
scenes of appalling suffering and abject misery
that brought tears to the eyes and a lump to
the throat,
yet I was no longer truly shocked
for I'd seen them before—
different people,
different emaciated bodies and haunted faces
yet the same scenes—
history repeating itself time and again.

We speak of making poverty history, Lord,
and we've done that,
but not in the way intended.
We've made it part of our world,
an accepted norm,
a fact of life . . . and death . . . for countless
millions,
and though it's not all our doing,
much of it down to forces beyond our control,
we're all still complicit in the crime,
none of us able to absolve ourselves fully
of responsibility.
Forgive the evil of our world,
and our share within it,
and give us all a common resolve to tackle poverty
and to consign it truly to history.
Amen.

The Alien

It was inhuman,
literally,
a monstrous creature from another world,
with no scruples, compassion, or feeling,
mutilating bodies and destroying lives
without even a shred of compunction.
But, of course, it wasn't real—
just a figment of the author's imagination:
an extraterrestrial dreamed up in the mind
and brought to life on the screen.

I saw more inhumanity,
more suffering and slaughter,
only this time it was all too real—
pictures on the television and in the papers
of unspeakable carnage,
lives cruelly shattered with equal lack
of compunction.
And it was no alien to blame,
but ordinary people,
fellow human beings,
who somehow saw murder as their mission,
killing as their calling.

Heal, Lord, our broken world,
and put an end to its madness,
so that, whatever divides,
we may see beyond cause or grievance
to the common humanity that unites us all.
Amen.

The Injury

It was a painstaking business,
the bones, shattered by the impact,
needing to be pieced together like a puzzle,
then carefully supported
while the breaks began to knit.
Would the injury heal,
the body mend?
We could only hope and pray.

Lord, our world lies equally broken,
fractured by prejudice,
splintered by hate,
scarred by fear,
and for all our efforts we cannot make it whole.
Pick up the pieces and bind them together,
bringing healing where there is hurt
and unity where there is division.
Hear our prayer
and honor our hopes.
Amen.

The Soup

We murmured appreciatively,
licking our lips in anticipation,
for the soup smelled good,
a perfect way to start the meal.
And though it was soon finished,
our bowls pushed aside,
no matter,
for it was just the first course—
plenty more to come.

Only suddenly, Lord,
I thought of the homeless person waiting in line at
the shelter
his ladle of soup not a starter
but the only meal he'd eat that day;
nothing fine or fancy about it,
yet to him a feast,
bringing a little succor to his ravaged body,
a respite from the winter's chill . . .
and I could eat no more,
my meal having lost its savor.
Teach me, Lord, in my plenty,
to remember those with so much less,
for should I forget them,
I forget you too.
Amen.

The Roadside Assistance Van

It was a common enough sight,
a roadside assistance van parked on the
hard shoulder,
lights flashing as its driver walked across
to the stricken vehicle,
but at that moment few sights were more welcome,
for the vehicle was ours
and we'd been waiting for what seemed an eterni-
ty for help to arrive.
No need to wait longer, though:
a tweak here and twiddle there
and the job was done,
the car fit again for us to complete our journey.

If only human hearts could be fixed so easily, Lord,
how special that would be,
but when lives are wrecked by sickness, fear,
hurt, and sorrow,
they can break down completely,
the business of repair a much longer process.
Reach out to all who feel they cannot carry on,
and give them strength not just to resume
their journey
but to embark on it with confidence renewed
and anticipation restored,
able to see it safely through until they reach
the end.
Amen.

The Second Helping

I didn't need any more,
for I was full already,
stuffed to the point of bursting,
but I couldn't resist another helping
the meal being delicious,
too good to turn down.
I regretted it later, though—
cursed myself for a fool,
since instead of being pleasurably content,
I felt bloated,
uncomfortable, to say the least.

I don't think of myself as a glutton, Lord,
but I am, sometimes,
eating far more than I need
while others go hungry.
Help me to recognize when enough is enough,
and instead of overfeeding myself
teach me to think of those not fed at all.
Amen.

The Cancer Patient

The treatment was hard enough to bear—
the hair loss, nausea, and pain—
and worse still was the fear,
not just of suffering and slow decline
but of being separated from loved ones;
of finally saying goodbye.
Yet hardest of all were the awkward silences,
forced smiles,
and well-meant platitudes—
being seen not as a person but a patient,
no longer an individual but a disease.

To all wrestling with terminal illness, Lord,
give the assurance that you will always value them
for who they are;
and help their families, friends, and colleagues
as they struggle to come to terms with *their*
feelings,
to do the same:
seeing not the illness but the individual underneath.
Whatever else may be lost,
may that continue,
to the end
and beyond.
Amen.

The Puzzle

There was a piece missing!
After all the effort I'd put in,
the painstaking hours of concentration,
I was left frustrated,
dismayed,
for the puzzle was incomplete.
Hard though I looked,
long though I searched,
it proved in vain;
the picture, it seemed,
condemned to remain unfinished.

For many, Lord, it's not a puzzle that's incomplete
but life itself.
For all their striving, they feel unfulfilled,
a component missing,
and though they can't quite place what it is,
they search hungrily for that special something,
that elusive final piece to complete the picture.
Draw near to them,
that in you they may find what they seek:
the One who satisfies our inner yearning,
and gives meaning to all.
Amen.

The Self-service Store

There was no one to serve me—
just a woman at the checkout,
waiting to add up my bill
and take my money.
And yes, I preferred it that way,
for it was quick and convenient,
giving me time to browse at leisure
and choose as I saw fit.
Yet it made me uneasy,
for it pointed beyond itself,
speaking of a society
where self-service is the norm rather than
the exception,
and looking after number one the only creed.

Lord, in a world where so many cannot fight
their corner;
where the rich prosper and the poor are crushed;
the strong thrive and the weak go to the wall;
where naked self-interest
leads to friendships being broken,
people estranged,
societies divided,
and nations driven to conflict,
teach me your way of love and humility,
of putting the interests of others before my own.
If I would serve *you*,
teach me to serve *all*.
Amen.

The Bridge

It spanned the divide,
allowing passage from one side to the other,
those formerly separated suddenly brought close,
the gulf skillfully bridged.

Lord, in a divided world,
where chasms of fear, hatred, envy, and injustice
come between so many,
help me to build bridges—
to do what I can,
where I can;
to construct links,
create dialogue,
and promote partnership,
bringing together those previously kept apart.
Where barriers estrange and rifts alienate,
help me to be a peacemaker.
Amen.

The Broken Window

One throw, that's all it took—
one stone hurled by a thoughtless child
and suddenly the window was shattered,
reduced to jagged shards and splintered glass.

So many, Lord, find their lives shattered—
broken by the loss of a loved one,
accident or injury,
the onset of disease,
or the breakdown of relationships—
and though sometimes they can be restored
and the pieces put back together,
sometimes they can't,
in this life, at least, the damage too great to mend.
Reach out into fragmented hearts,
bringing healing and hope,
until that day when your kingdom comes,
and all is made whole.
Amen.

The Terrorist Attack

It was carnage,
sickening and horrific,
like a scene out of hell—
injuries too awful to contemplate,
lives, like the twisted wreckage around them,
shattered beyond repair.
A morning full of promise
had become the stuff of nightmares,
yet it was all too real.

Where were you, Lord, when it happened?
What were you thinking of?
How could you let it be?
I look for answers,
yet search in vain,
the quest raising more questions than it solves;
but if one thing is clear, it's that here,
in this mindless maiming and murder,
we need you more than ever.
Come to our broken, bleeding world, Lord,
and bind up its wounds.
Assure us, despite how things seem,
that hope is mightier than fear,
right stronger than wrong,
and love greater than all.
Amen.

The HIV/AIDS Patient

They avoided him,
shrinking back when he approached,
well aware the response was foolish,
but controlled by half-formed fears,
suspicion and prejudice that formed
a wall between them.
No comment was made—
none was needed:
he walked forlornly away,
condemned to carry his burden alone.

Some say it's a punishment, Lord,
a sign of your anger.
Others pity him.
Most keep their distance.
But not you.
As you touched the untouchables
throughout your ministry,
so you reach out still,
seeing not the affliction
but the person underneath.
Forgive, Lord, the feebleness of our love,
and teach us to do the same.
Amen.

The Tire and Exhaust Center

I didn't have time to hang around,
nor money to waste, come to that,
so the center was ideal for my needs,
allowing me to pop in with no appointment
and have both exhaust and tires replaced,
the job tackled on the spot,
problem solved.

When I look at the world, Lord—
its tensions and suffering,
need and heartbreak—
it's hard not to wonder what you're doing
and why you take so long to put things right,
for so much within it seems to question your love
and undermine your will.
Help me to understand, though,
that there are no quick fixes or short-term solutions,
but that you are working nonetheless,
your purpose destined to triumph,
not in *my* time
but in *yours*.
Amen.

The Clowns

It was the usual slapstick stuff,
predictable to say the least,
but the kids loved it,
roaring their approval,
rolling about in glee.
They saw the mask, that's all,
the painted smile,
and why not?—
there'd be time enough in later years
to understand the tears.

Remind me, Lord, that what I see of others
is rarely the whole story;
that behind the façade,
beneath the veneer,
most of them wrestle with their secret pain,
hidden fears,
and inner turmoil—
casualties of the hustle and bustle of life.
Teach me that beneath the public face
there lies a private world,
and help me in all my dealings to allow for both.
Amen.

The Board of Trustees

It was an honor,
but an onerous one,
the future of thousands
dependent on their stewardship,
for the resources they administered were held
on trust,
representing not just assets but people—
their savings and investments,
lives and livelihoods.

You've honored *us*, Lord,
each and every one,
placing in our care not just land or money
but the world itself,
an asset beyond price.
Forgive my share in squandering its resources,
living today with no thought of tomorrow.
Forgive my betrayal of your trust,
living with little thought
for present and future generations.
Teach me to live wisely,
mindful of all your creation,
and grant that others may do the same.
Amen.

The Hose Ban

There was no crisis yet,
no cause for alarm,
but reservoirs were low,
the drought starting to bite,
and, with no rain forecast,
the water supply had to be used with care.
Yet when the ban was announced, folk were up
in arms,
out for blood . . .
for they couldn't water their gardens or wash
their cars!

I think, Lord, of the millions in this world
who would gladly swap places—
those for whom *any* water is a luxury.
I think of dehydrated children, dying of thirst;
of communities whose supplies
are polluted and diseased,
of lands parched,
pasture turned to dust.
And I'm ashamed,
for like so many I'm swift to bemoan my lot
and slow to count my blessings.
Teach me to understand how lucky I am
and to think, for a change, of others instead
of myself.
Amen.

The Vitamin Tablets

Did I need them?
Probably not,
but I took them anyway,
better safe than sorry.
I ate well enough, truth be told,
but why leave anything to chance?
For, after all,
few things matter more than health.

Teach me, Lord, how lucky I am
compared to millions across the world;
so many having barely enough to survive,
let alone the good things I take for granted.
Teach me to focus on their *needs* rather than
my *extras*
and to realize that through giving a little
I can bring them *much.*
Amen.

The Suitcase

He gasped,
struggling with the load,
veins knotted on his brow
and sweat dripping down his cheeks—
his progress like that of a convict
wrestling with heavy shackles.
Repeatedly he paused to rest,
stretching aching fingers and weary arms,
and I feared for him—
a man his age with such a burden to carry.

Lord, he is not alone,
for we all carry baggage through life,
staggering under a burden of guilt,
a weight of remorse,
a crushing load of fear.
Yet we have no need,
for you are ready to carry
what we can never shoulder alone.
Teach us in turn to let go
and walk unencumbered,
trusting that you hold everything,
even us,
in the palm of your hand.
Amen.

The Frayed Rope

It had been strong once,
easily able to bear the load and take the strain,
but the rope now was frayed—
serviceable,
but only just:
the question not *if* it would snap
but *when*.

It reminded me, Lord, of people,
so many worn to breaking point,
ground down by sickness, hurt, worry, and fear,
by the ravages of time,
and uncertain how much longer they can cope.
Reach out to strengthen and restore,
from the tangled threads of their lives
weaving cords that will not be broken.
Amen.

The Dump

They dug through the garbage
like eager parasites,
sifting through the piles of waste
and setting aside item after item for further use.
What others counted as rubbish, they valued,
knowing it could be restored,
recycled,
reused.

In a world, Lord,
where so many feel left on the scrap heap,
discarded by society and of no use to anyone,
teach me to see the worth not just of objects
but equally of people.
Open my eyes to look more deeply,
recognizing the gifts, qualities, and potential
of those around me,
and, wherever I can, help me to nurture them,
so that they may bloom again.
Remind me that *you* value everyone,
even if others don't,
and help me to do the same.
Amen.

The Oil Slick

It wasn't quite the disaster of old,
for advances had been made,
technology yielding ways to contain the spill
and limit the damage,
but the oil was there nonetheless:
choking, killing, soiling, polluting,
leaving a stain on all it touched—
so swift to form,
so hard to remove.

Our world is stained, Lord,
engulfed by a black tide of injustice, intolerance,
fear, and hatred
that desecrates and destroys countless lives
and, for all our so-called advances,
we're no nearer to containing it than we've
ever been.
Come to our aid,
and cleanse us of all that denies and divides—
that precludes joy and crushes hope.
Transform what we can never change ourselves,
and make all things new.
Amen.